Counting

By John Satchwell
Illustrated by Katy Sleight

PUBLISHED BY
DISCOVERY TOYS

one
body

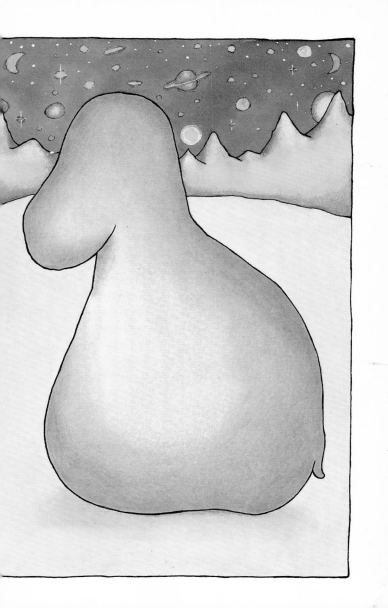

two
eyes

3

three
horns

4

four
legs

five
teeth

six
spikes

seven
spots

eight
holes

nine
flags

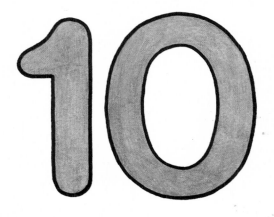

ten
friends

1 one

2 two

3 three

4 four

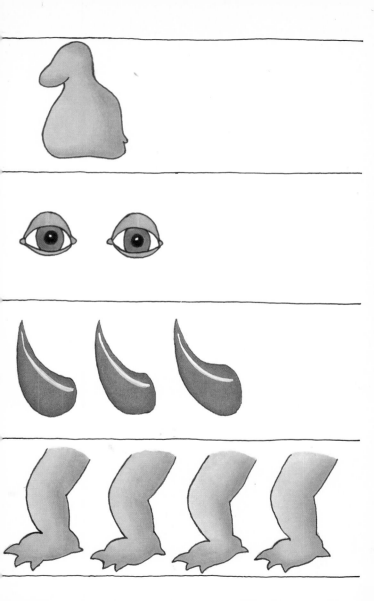

5 five

6 six

7 seven

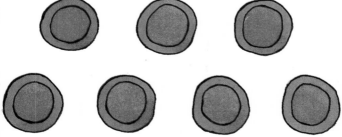

8 eight

9 nine

10 ten